Blues Lang

The Language of the Blu

Blues Language

The Language of the Blues Guitar Masters

ISBN: 978-1499579239

Copyright © 2013 Sam Smiley

The moral right of this author has been asserted.
All rights reserved. No part of this publication may be reproduced, stored in a retrieval system, or transmitted in any form or by any means, without the prior permission in writing of the publisher. The publisher is not responsible for websites (or their content) that are not owned by the publisher.

The musical notations and audio included with this book is the interpretation of the author and constitutes fair use in the context of musical education.

www.samsmileymusic.com/

All the audio examples in this book are available for free download from

http://www.samsmileymusic.com/bluesaudio/

Contents

I. Introduction 4

II. Vocabulary 6

III. Blues Sections 8

IV. Techniques 11

V. Blues Progressions 13

    Other Forms 16

VI. The Players 19

VII. The I Chord 22

VIII. The IV Chord 43

IX. The V Chord 53

X. Turnaround 63

XI. Endings 70

XII. Etude Solos 75

    Etude #1 76

    Etude #2 77

    Variations 78

XIII. Discography 79

Conclusion 80

    About Sam Smiley 80

Appendix 81

    The I Chord 81

    The IV Chord 88

    The V Chord 90

    Turnaround 91

    Ending 91

Contact Details 92

I. Introduction

The blues is the foundation of every American music style in the 20th century. Rock, jazz, country, roots, everything came out of the blues tradition that started in the early 20th century.

This book is a study of some of the great electric guitarists' phrases and vocabulary. The Chicago and Texas blues traditions are the main sources for the licks here.

When learning music, it is important to learn musical phrases, licks, and ideas from the masters. Blues is no different.

One advantage the blues has is that the form is generally the same from tune to tune. Another is the ease to "sound good" using the minor pentatonic or blues scale. These can also be disadvantages because many players tend to play the same thing no matter where they are in the form or which tune they are playing.

Thinking in terms of *vocabulary* and *context* helps to solve this issue. The basic idea is that each section of the blues has specific vocabulary and licks that work in that section. Placing licks in the proper context will help you to sound like an authentic, legit blues player.

Placing licks in the right place shouldn't be the end of your blues education though. The second step in this process is to absorb those sounds and licks and make them your own. This can be done by experimentation, using different fingerings, forcing into songs, or just by absorbing them by practicing.

The goal should be infusing your own playing with the vocabulary of the masters and creating your own take on it. Think of great authors – they still use a language and format, but are creative within those contexts. Many of the great innovators started out by mastering one form before creating another one entirely.

Many musicians tend to think, "Won't I sound just like…."? What would be the problem sounding too much like B.B. King or Buddy Guy?

Forging your own sound is a noble thing to do, and it is great to go after that goal. It is important to keep some of the language in your playing as a point of departure.

Organization

With this idea in mind, this book is organized by section of the blues. I have broken down the main form into five sections.

The I (one) chord - This section is the most common and most used section. There are at least 7 bars in the blues form that are played with the I chord. These licks can also be used in other parts of the form.

The IV (four) chord - Many times the IV chord is approached in a completely different way than the others. This is the section that really helped me *hear* the differences in sections.

The V (five) chord - The V chord is the section at bars 9 and 10. Generally this section also contains a IV chord, but some songs use it as a long V chord in many cases. Soloists also tend to build tension in this section.

The Turnaround- The turnaround is the last 2 bars of the form. It brings the player back to top of the form. Many of these licks are very similar. Players should start here to get immediate results in sounding "authentic".

Endings – Endings are extremely important. Many players tend to over look the endings. The players who know endings sound authentic very quickly.

The Licks

The licks in this book are the language of the blues greats. You can find many similarities in these licks between players, but it's very interesting to find the vast differences. Each lick is presented in its original key.

One approach to learning this material is to study the vocabulary of specific players (such as B.B. King or Buddy Guy). Another way to go about it would be to work on each section one at a time.

A third way, which might be the most effective, would be to create your own "etudes" from the licks. The chapter "Solos Etudes" details this process and has a few examples. Etudes are great ways to absorb this material because they are real world examples instead of playing isolated licks.

All the audio examples in this book are available for free download from

http://www.samsmileymusic.com/bluesaudio/

II. Vocabulary

When many guitar players start to "solo" they are usually taught to start with scales. The scale approach can be a quick way to get some useable sounds that will work over the blues.

But that sound gets really old pretty quickly because using a scale for an entire solo lacks direction and voice leading. I'm not saying that the blues masters necessarily thought of the fact that there was not any voice leading, but I am certain they could tell by musical instinct that they needed to use something other than just scales.

So how do you go beyond scales and play something musical?

The goal should be developing *vocabulary* instead of scales. The idea behind vocabulary is that playing a musical style is similar to speaking a language. Conversations are made up from words and groups of words, not from letters and punctuation. Sure, it's important to understand spelling, letters, and grammar, but it is not the key to communication. Vocabulary is.

To apply this idea to music we have to think of things like scales and arpeggios as the letters and grammar. The vocabulary is made up of short phrases that are commonly played. This entire book is based on the idea of vocabulary.

You will find that focusing on vocabulary instead of scales will bring a new level of authenticity and depth to your playing. It is really the key to sounding like you know what you are doing.

Think of a child learning to speak. They might start by imitating words they hear all around them but get many wrong. After trying this for a while they may start to get a few (mama, dada, yes, no…). They then learn more and more words as they grow, adding every day to their vocabulary.

Once they start trying to form sentences they still might get some words slightly wrong but they are still communicating. They might even use some words in the wrong context altogether. Over the years they finally get to a point where they're communicating effectively-sometimes over many years. The crazy thing is that during those first few years they probably only know the alphabet as a song, if even that.

The process in music is very similar. Hopefully it will not take several years to get it down!

Instead of starting with phonics and the alphabet start by trying to make words you hear from others (recordings). This book has 125 phrases to get you started.

Once you have a few of these together you should try to string them together to make a musical thought. Still not paying attention yet to the scale or theory behind it. It's just raw music still at this point. Again, you'll make mistakes and that's ok. Using your vocabulary out of order or trying to force new "words" into places they don't belong yet are all natural processes of learning to speak the language.

The next step is to really get into grammar or context of the music. Think of grammar as where you're placing the words and how you connect them. The more music you get into the more you find where and when the licks work. The licks presented here are organized by the section of the blues form that they are played over. It's not just about knowing the vocabulary but how and where to use it!

Eventually you'll begin to speak the language of blues. You are putting things where they belong, using the right words, and maybe even bringing your own thing to the conversation. Great!

NOW is a great time to start trying to really infuse your personality and create something original. You've probably already been adding your in personality, but really focusing on originality and personality is really effective once you can speak a musical language effectively.

III. Blues Sections

Most blues tunes have very similar changes. You may have even experienced playing in a jam session where players say, "it's a blues in G," and everyone can play it. That's a good way to get through a gig or jam, but it's a much more effective to get deeper into the form of the blues. "

Many players will approach a solo by using the blues and minor pentatonic scales. That approach works well, but sometimes leaves little to be desired. When I would play blues I would just use the scales and it just sounded bland. So I went back to the drawing board and listened. As I listened to several B.B. King songs I noticed he would do certain things every time on the IV chord. He would also play certain phrases on the turnarounds. This lead me to thinking of the blues as a deeper form than a collection of chords that I can paste a scale onto.

As you start thinking of the blues this way it becomes helpful to think of the blues divided into sections that are pretty much the same in function and chord changes from tune to tune. In fact, identifying the sections actually helps you to distinguish and track differences between specific songs.

The I Chord

This first section is the I chord. The ease of "sounding good" on this chord along with the length of the chord make it a common place for many players to show off rather than create meaningful music.

So how do you avoid this pitfall?

The answer is to create great melodies. As you look at the licks, you will find that the commonality is the strength of a melody.

What makes a strong melody?

Well that's a million dollar question. BUT there are a few things that are pretty easy to find in these melodies.

They are melodies *first* and guitar licks *second*.

This is a big key because many guitarists think of licks and guitar tricks. The good news is that if you focus on melody and musicality, you automatically set yourself apart. B.B. King does a great job of this. Many of his licks are not technically challenging but are very strong melodies.

The sound of the chord is well stated and clear.

This means that these players distinguish the chord tones, an approach usually reserved for jazz guitarists. If the key is C, you want to focus on some of the triad notes-like C, E, and G and play melodies that highlight these notes.

They are rhythmically clear.

Most good music teachers will, at some point, tell you that the most important thing is the rhythm. This concept holds up too when talking about strong melodies and the blues. Each of these players undoubtedly *play* rhythms very well, but that's not what I'm talking about here.

This idea centers on the fact that the melodies are strong and follow the natural cadence of rhythm. These basic rules really can't be written down, but you glean them from listening to a lot of music and playing a lot of music from the greats – no matter the style.

The Movable Lick

The I chord licks are probably the most versatile. They can be moved to really any other section of the blues and still sound good. The I chord licks can form a really good basic understanding of blues vocabulary.

The IV chord

The IV chord takes place in bars 5 and 6. The biggest distinguishing note in the IV chord is the 3rd of the chord. Again if we're in C, the IV chord is F – which means the 3rd of the chord would be A. So in order to "hit the changes" you want to make sure to highlight the A note in these bars.

Another note that changes is the 7th. The 7th is a half step lower than the I chord's 3. Back to our C example: C's 3rd is E, while F's 7th would be Eb. Billy Butler plays a great lick that shows this relationship.

The IV chord also briefly returns in the 10th bar. Usually that bar is with the V chord, but sometimes a IV chord lick will work well there too.

The V Chord

The V chord typically brings us back to the tonic. In classical music this is called the dominant function chord. It makes us want to hear the I chord again.

In this book the V chord section refers to bars 9 & 10. Sometimes this is only the V chord, other times you hear the IV chord in bar 10. But since this book is about the *function* of each section instead of the chord changes we will look at both chords together.

Turnaround

The blues is usually repeated several times, especially when someone is soloing. The section of the tune that brings us back to the beginning is called the turnaround. It is usually a I chord followed by the V.

This section is the clearest place to hear the vocabulary idea in action. Most of the players in this study play lines that end on the 5th note of the scale. This is a place where all the greatest blues players use very similar phrases.

Endings

Endings are pretty self-explanatory. It's the end of a tune. This is another place where you can clearly hear vocabulary. Each player has a number of licks to use to end songs.

Endings are a vital part to playing gigs and it's important to have a deep "bag" to draw from when ending tunes.

IV. Techniques

The blues lays on the guitar very easily, which is probably one of the major reasons that it became the most commonly played instrument in the style. There are a few things that are unique to the guitar that should be addressed before we dive into the vocabulary.

Fingerings

Many of the licks do fall within the scale fingerings. This does not mean that the players were started with scales, but that the licks fell within the notes in the scales.

Most guitarists have learned the minor pentatonic box shape in Fig 1. This one is very commonly used with the middle strings (D, G, and B strings).

Figure 1

There is a second fingering that is commonly used by blues guitarists. You can hear/see this fingering in many of the licks by Albert King and Freddie King.

The second fingering shares the 8th fret notes on the E and B strings with the original fingering. See Figure 2 below.

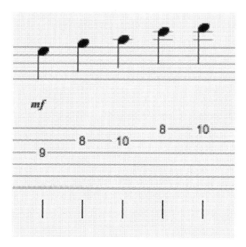

Bending

Bending is an extremely important technique in blues guitar. Here are a few tips on bending.
Make sure you are wrapping your thumb around the top of the neck (near the low E string). This helps you to squeeze the strings instead of pushing them.

Check the tuning of the bend. Bends are not just inflections, they are a way to go from one pitch to another. Make sure you know your target pitch and check it.

Use fingers behind your fretting finger to support the bend.

When making larger bends (see Albert King) try using momentum to reach the pitch. In other words, make these bends quick bends instead of slowly trying to reach for the correct pitch.

Go for it! Try not to over think bending and just go for it. Keep going for it even when your fingertips begin to hurt a bit. Calluses will form and get strong with use.

V. Blues Progressions

The blues is one of the easiest styles to use to jam because it has a common chord progression that most guitarists and other musicians know very well. There are several different variations of the form though, and we will take a look at some of them.

Standard 12 Bar Blues

The standard 12 bar blues is the basic form that the other sets of changes are derived from.

Figure 2

Figure 2 shows the basic blues form in the key of C. You can also look at the form by looking at the degree of the scale each chord is from. To look at the progression this way, first number the chords.

C	Dm	Em	F	G	Am	Bdim
I	ii	iii	IV	V	vi	vii

The progression can then be described using the Roman numerals. This is very similar using the "Nashville Number System" – which is the same but uses Arabic numbers instead of Roman numerals. This helps to understand the progression regardless of key.

I	I	I	I
IV	IV	I	I
V	V	I	V

Variations

The first and most common variation is to put a IV chord on the second measure. Figure 6 shows the first 4 bars with this variation.

Figure 3

A second variation is to put a IV chord in the 10th bar. This one is used very frequently.

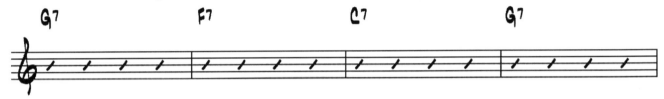

Figure 4

If you put these two variations in the progression you will get the chords in Figure 8. This is one of the most common ways to play the blues changes.

I	IV	I	I
IV	IV	I	I
V	IV	I	V

Jazz Blues

The blues makes up a very large percentage of changes for jazz tunes. In fact, in many schools and educational systems the blues is the first progression taught to learn improvisation. The jazz blues differs slightly from the basic blues progression.

The first difference happens in bar 6, where the sharp IV diminished chord is used. This leads back to the I chord.

Another major difference is the use of the VI chord. Another way to look at the VI chord is to think of it as the V chord leading to the ii. This is also called *secondary dominant*. This comes up in bars 8 and again in the turnaround.

Finally, the jazz blues uses a ii chord in measures 9 and again in the turnaround. Figure 9 shows a break down of the jazz blues and basic blues forms. Figure 10 shows the jazz blues in the key of C.

I	IV	I	I
IV	#IV	I	VI
ii	V	I VI	ii V

Figure 5

Stormy Monday

T-Bone Walker's classic, "Stormy Monday" has another set of changes that can be a lot of fun to play over. This tune has both chromatic movements and diatonic (or within the key) movements.

I   IV   I bII   I
IV   IV   I ii   iii IV
Vsus bVI   I IV   I V

Figure 6

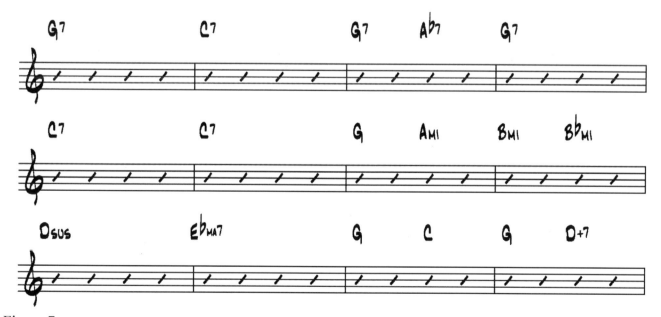

Figure 7

Other Forms

8 Bar Blues

The blues is often played using an 8 bar form. This form has many variations and we will take a look at two common forms.

The first variation of 8 bar blues basically shortens the I and V chord sections by half. Figure 13 has the changes in the key of C.

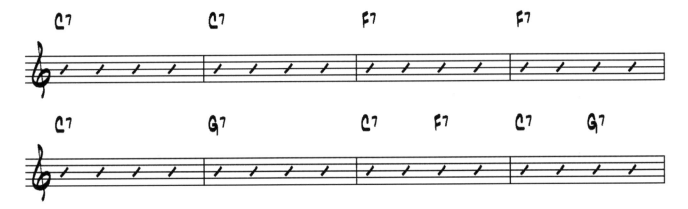

Figure 8

A second variation we will look at changes the blues form completely. In this variation the V chord comes in the 4th bar and the IV chord comes in the 6th bar. It is a great change of pace variation of the changes.

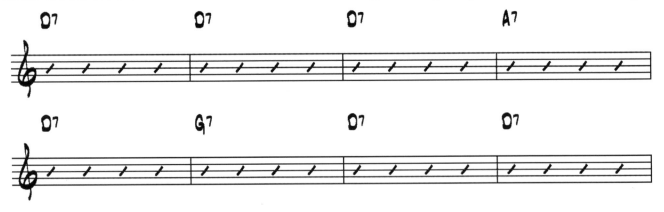

Figure 9

16 Bar Blues

The blues can also be extended to more than 12 bars. Many blues use a 16 bar form. Again, there are many variations of 16 bar blues forms, but most include extending the I chord. In figure 13, the I chord lasts twice as long while the rest of the form uses the standard 12 bar blues form.

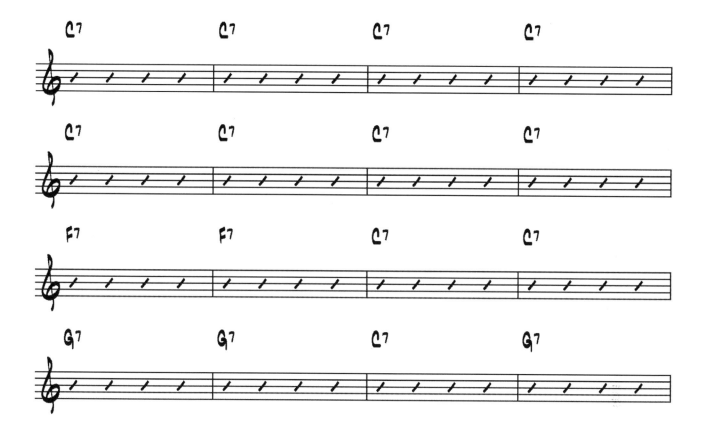

15 Bar Blues

The blues even takes on unconventional forms. The final example here is the 15 bar blues. In this example the form starts on the IV chord, which lasts three bars. The I chord follows for two bars. That 5 bar section is repeated. The form ends with two bars of the V chord followed by four bars of the I chord.

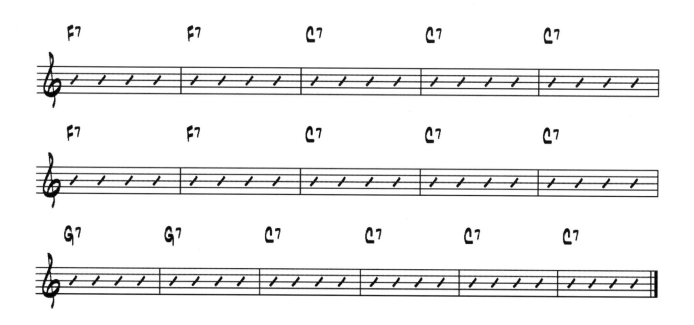

Using a different number of bars should not just be an exercise in musicianship. These unconventional forms usually happen because of the way the lyrics lay out, though they are great ways to help get a fresh take on your blues playing.

Play the Songs

While these variations on the blues changes are relatively easy to memorize, it is important to play the changes that go with the particular *song* you are playing. Many times players will "just play a blues" without really paying attention to the details of the form.

Most blues tunes have small, minor differences. One might go to the IV chord on bar 2 and another might stay on the V chord for bars 9 and 10. The point is that the small differences in chord changes make big differences in the sound of the song. In order to really get deep into the style it is important to actually play the changes that go with each song.

VI. The Players

Duane Allman

Duane Allman is a great blues guitarist, but is also a stunning slide player. Allman was a true student of the blues, studying Bobby Blue Bland, T-Bone Walker, B.B. King, and more growing up. His slide playing grew out of Elmore James, but Allman took it to a different level. His work with the Allman Brothers is great, but also check out his work with other artists such as Wilson Picket and Aretha Franklin.

Kenny Burrell

Kenny Burrell is known as a jazz guitarist. He was one of the 1960s guitarists who were right in the middle of the meeting point between blues and jazz. Kenny Burrell made a name for himself playing with great organist, Jimmy Smith. He usually played a large hollow body guitar and kept his bending to a minimum.

Billy Butler

Billy Butler is a lesser known guitarist. He put jazz and soul with the blues together to come up with an interesting sound on the blues. His tone is very mellow and he plays things that are a little outside the box.

Eric Clapton

Clapton's name has been synonymous with English blues since the mid 1960s when he was playing with the Yardbirds. He went on to record very influential albums with John Mayall, form the classic rock powerhouse Cream, and have a solo career that has lasted 4 decades. Every few years Clapton returns to classic blues and records some unbelievable music.

Albert Collins

Texas blues great Collins is called "The Iceman" is well known for being a telecaster player. His playing has a different vibe to it because some of the tunings he uses, including D minor. Many of his songs have references to ice and frost. Collins says the nickname came after seeing 'defrost' in a friend's car and thinking that it would be a good word to create a persona after.

Buddy Guy

Buddy Guy is the quintessential Chicago Blues guitarist. He was a sideman for Muddy Waters and Junior Wells. He has also since had a very long career as a solo artist.

Pat Hare

Pat Hare is best known as the guitarist for blues legend, Bobby "Blue" Bland on the song "Farther Up the Road". He used a very distorted sound but played some of the greatest blues lines recorded. He was also a member of Muddy Waters' band for many years.

Earl Hooker

Known for being one of the Chicago scene's greatest guitarists, Earl Hooker is a guitarists' guitarist with players such as Buddy Guy singing his praises. He is also known as a great slide player.

Elmore James

Elmore James is the quintessential slide guitar player. His slide playing has influenced just about every guitarist since who picks up a slide. His song, "Dust My Broom" has spawned a lick that is so intrinsically connected with the blues that it is hard to imagine slide guitar playing without it. James was a huge influence on Duane Allman as well as countless other guitarists.

Albert King

Albert King is one of the most important blues players in history because of his huge influence on rock guitarists. His trademark has always been his bends, especially the minor 3rd or 2 step bends. King used open tunings which left the strings slightly looser in order to facilitate the bends. Albert King was an enormous influence on Stevie Ray Vaughn.

B.B. King

B.B.'s style is sometimes misunderstood as simple but he could really play some difficult things. He influenced a multitude of guitarists and set the bar very high for those who followed.

B.B. King's style is very melodic with techniques like bends working to enhance melodies. He rarely did anything for the sake of doing it, everything you hear has a purpose and helps support the melodies he plays.

Freddie King

Another one of Chicago's greatest guitarists was none other than Freddie King. He had a big influence on rock guitarists (similar to Albert King). He wrote the song "Hideaway", which was one of Eric Clapton's biggest hits early in his career.

Magic Sam

Magic Sam is best known as a West Side of Chicago blues guitarist. His playing defines the style. He is the writer of the classic "Sweet Home Chicago."

Pat Martino

Martino has been known as a jazz guitarist his entire career, but he cut his teeth playing in the organ groups led by Jack McDuff and others. His jazz playing is impeccable, but he infuses it with great blues licks.

Wes Montgomery

Wes is one of the greatest jazz guitarists to ever play the instrument. He is known for using his thumb to pluck the strings, which gives him a very mellow but punchy sound. Wes had the influence of the blues on just about every recording he made, and went on to influence guitarists in all genres since.

Jimmy Rogers

Jimmy Rogers is a lesser-known great from the Chicago scene. He came from Muddy Water's tree of musicians and played lead guitar with Waters. He was also a bandleader on Chess records throughout the 1950s and 960s.

Otis Rush

Otis Rush was one of the "west side of Chicago" guitarists (along with Magic Sam and Buddy Guy). Some even speculate that he was the most talented player of the style, but had enough career twisting events that he was never really known as well as the others.

Stevie Ray Vaughn

Stevie Ray Vaughn helped to bring blues back to the masses in the early and mid 1980s. His tone and technique have been legendary. Albert King was one of SRV's biggest influences.

T-Bone Walker

T-Bone is easily one of the most important electric guitarists. His style set the tone for all electric blues that followed. His main influence was Charlie Christian, who also helped set the tone for all *electric guitar* that came after him.

Muddy Waters

Muddy Waters is one of the fathers of Chicago blues. While his recordings eventually defined the style, he started in the Mississippi Delta. After moving to Chicago, he became well known for his slide playing. He played in or led bands with many of Chicago blues' greatest players.

Don't forget, all the audio examples in this book are available for free download from

http://www.samsmileymusic.com/bluesaudio/

VII. The I Chord

The I chord is the most important chord to learn to solo over. It is the tonal center of the tune and is the chord heard most often in the progression.

Typically the I chord happens from bars 1 to 4. Other times the progression might move to a IV chord on bar 2, but the majority of electric blues use the I chord for all 4 measures. The I chord also comes back in bars 7 and 8 before moving to the V chord. Finally, it resolves the progression in bar 11.

All three of these places are places where the progression *moves to*, meaning the chords are structured in a way that lead the ear to resolve on the I chord. If you look at improvisation or melody writing from a perspective of tension and release, the I chord is the release point.

When practicing and learning these licks, try moving them around to different places on the neck. They appear in the key originally were played in.

Though they were all played over a I chord, they sound at home at any point in the progression.

The Licks

All of the licks are listed by artist and key so that you can get a feel for each artist's vocabulary. Some of the licks contain commentary to highlight interesting parts of the lick.

Duane Allman

Lick 1: Key of D

Duane Allman was a master of the slide guitar and blues. This lick was originally performed with a slide and in open E tuning, but sounds great in standard tuning without the slide. Check out the chromatic move leading up the b7th in the first bar. He then ends the lick with some nice slides. In the open tuning this lick happens all on the same fret. In standard tuning the lick still lays out pretty well.

Lick 2: Key of D

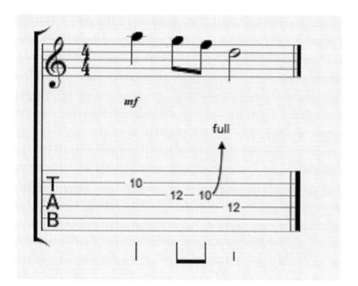

Lick 3: Key of A

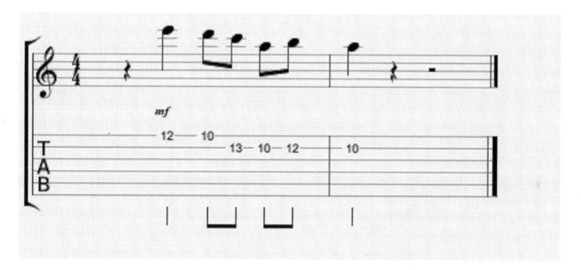

Billy Butler

Lick 4: Key of F

This is a very interesting lick from Billy Butler. Notice the use of bending the 2nd of the scale up to the flat 3rd, and then the 6th up to the flat 7th.

Lick 5: Key of F

This lick moves around the neck quite a bit. The idea is using double stop thirds with a chord tone as the highest note – the notes in an F chord are F, A, and C.

Kenny Burrell

Lick 6: Key of C

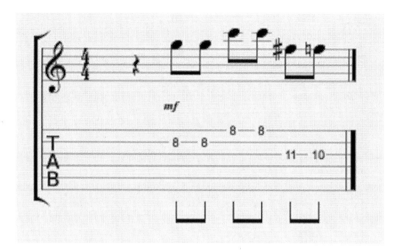

Lick 7: Key of C

This lick shows Kenny Burrell's expert use of the smaller bends. Many jazz guitarists use very thick strings so they don't bend quite as much as the blues guitarists. Still KB makes great use of bending from the flat 3rd to the major 3rd.

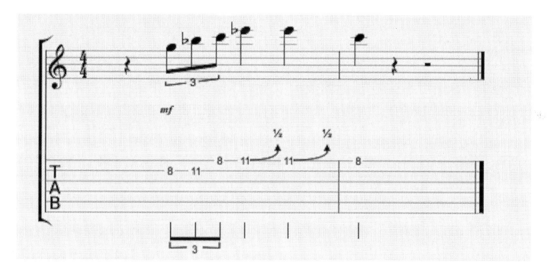

Eric Clapton

Lick 8: Key of C

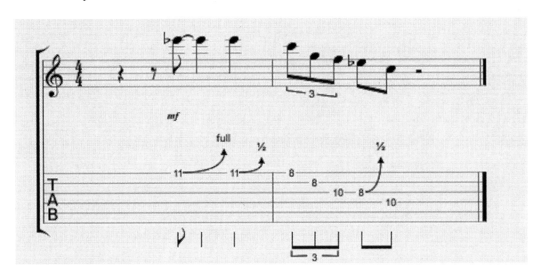

Lick 9: Key of C

This lick from Clapton has an interesting double bend and release. Pick only the first note and last one, the others should be part of the bend or the pull off.

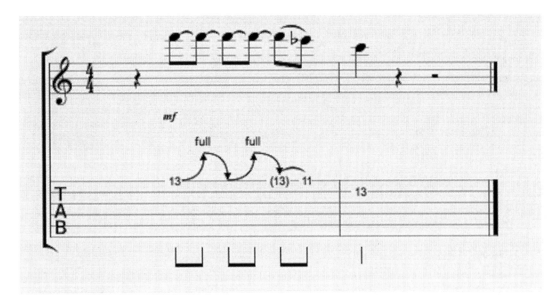

Albert Collins

Lick 10: Key of D

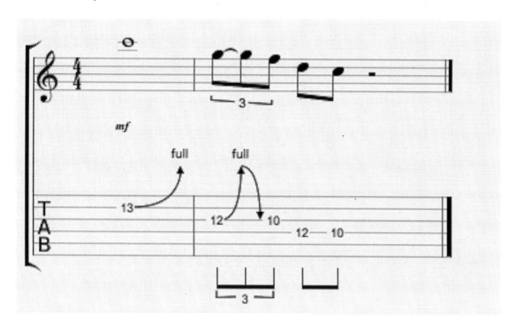

Lick 1: Key of D

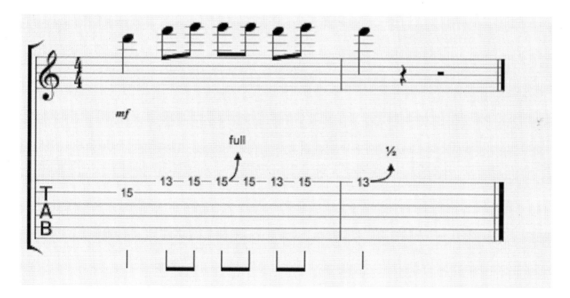

Buddy Guy

Lick 12: Key of A

This lick is a variation of the classic T-Bone Walker lick, this time moving backward through the notes.

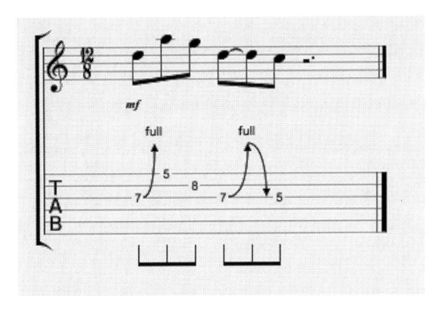

Lick 13: Key of F

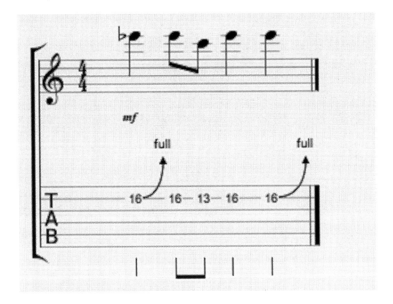

Lick 14: Key of F

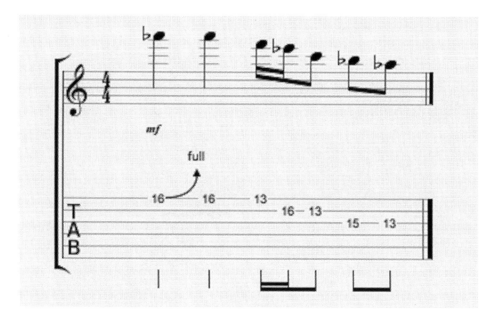

Lick 15: Key of F

This lick is part of a repeated lick where he repeats this phrase 4 times. The lick is played in straight 8ths instead of swing or shuffle. To play the double stops at the beginning, barre your ring finger at the 16th fret and first finger at the 13th fret.

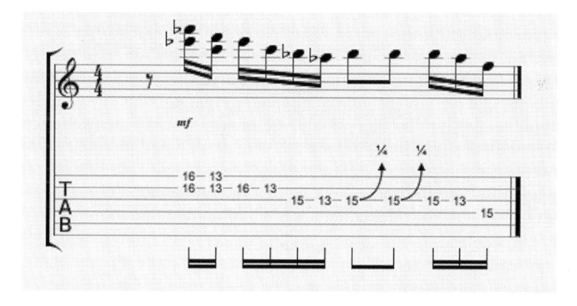

Pat Hare

Lick 16: Key of F

Lick 17: Key of F

Both this lick and Lick 16 from Pat Hare are easily within the normal "box" shape minor pentatonic scale. This one ends with the natural third, breaking out of that mould just enough at the end to give it some character.

Earl Hooker

Lick 18: Key of D

This Earl Hooker lick is based on using the 6th interval. Play this one using middle finger on the G string notes and first finger on the E string notes.

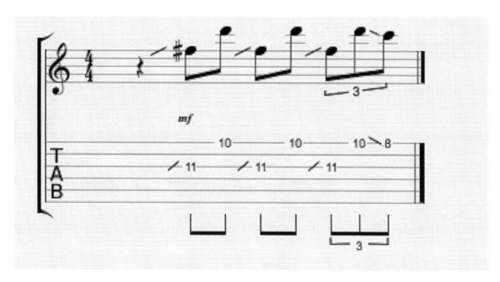

Elmore James

Lick 19: Key of D

Lick 20: Key of D

This lick is the classic "Dust My Broom" lick. Again, this is a slide lick arranged for non-slide guitar. Make sure to give the F in the second bar a slight bend to emulate the slide.

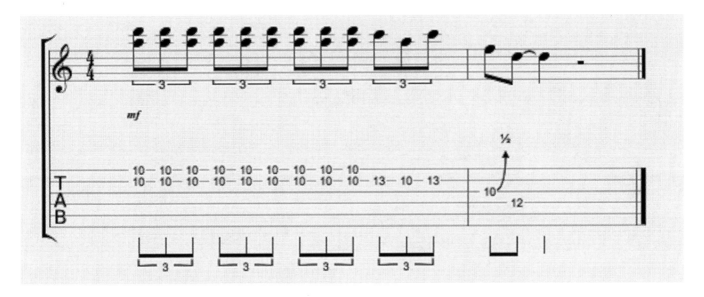

Albert King

Lick 21: Key of Bb

Play the last bar of this lick with a staccato C#.

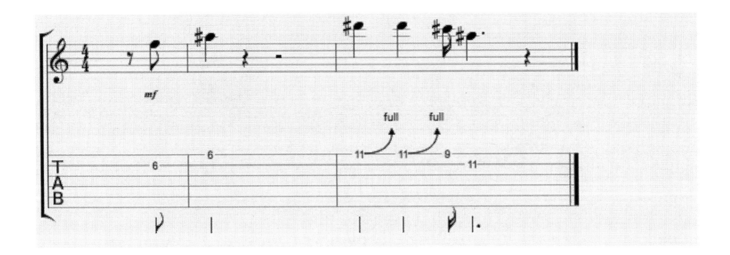

Lick 22: Key of Bb

This extended lick features a great triad run in the third bar. Again, notice how often the 6th degree (G) is used in the lick.

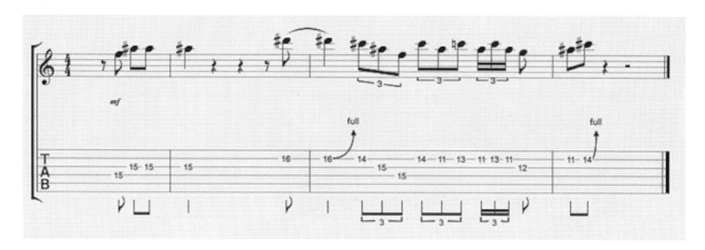

Lick 23: Key of C#

This lick has some of Albert King's signature 2 step bends. Albert would use different tunings in order to facilitate the bends but they are possible in standard tuning by putting a lot of momentum into the bend. You will not need a lot of strength, but try to get a lot of momentum when you first make the bend.

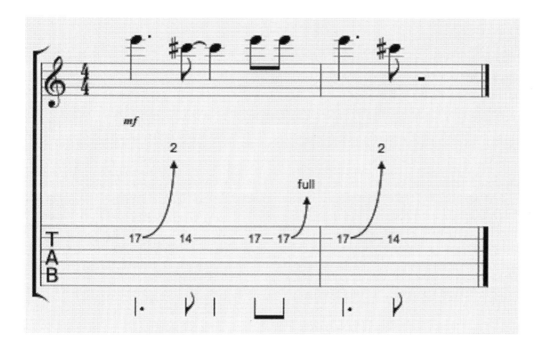

Lick 24: Key of C#

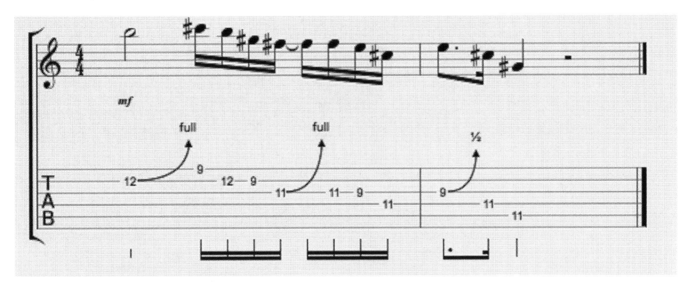

B.B. King

Lick 25: Key of C#

This lick is in the key of C#. It starts with a cliché line that has been used in volumes of solos. The ending is very interesting as he bends the 5th of the scale up to the 6th note (the 13th fret note on beat 3). Then he resolves the lick with the major 3rd.

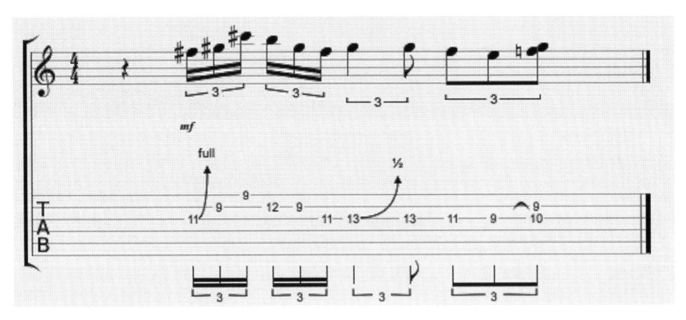

Lick 26: Key of C#

This lick comes from the same tune. Again, he uses a cliché to begin the lick but ends interestingly. Check out the sus chord on beat 4 of the first measure. Then he resolves it similar to Lick 25.

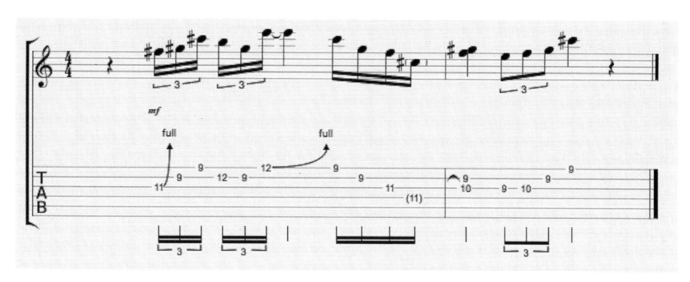

Lick 27: Key of C#

This lick starts with a great tritone double stop with the flat 3rd and 6th of the key.

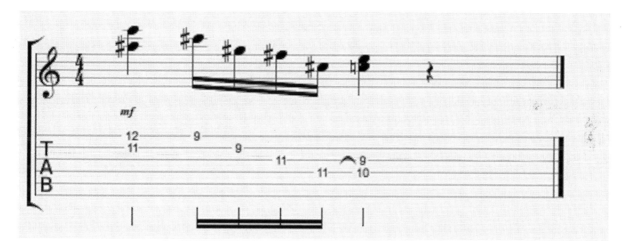

Lick 28: Key of Bb

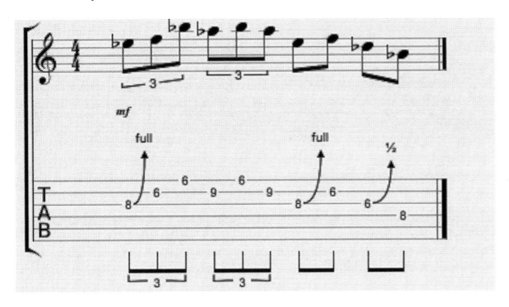

Lick 29: Key of D

This lick is based on the second scale shape in the scale chapter. The bends make this lick interesting, especially the bend from the flatted 3rd to the major 3rd at the end. He also uses the 6th frequently.

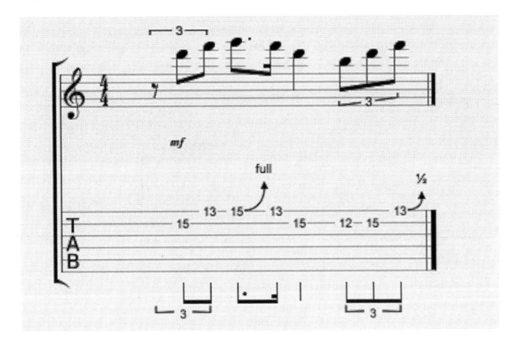

Freddie King

Lick 30: Key of D

Freddie King forms much of the base for rock and roll guitar playing. This lick is evidence of that as he skips from the flat 7th to the bent 4th note of the scale at the end of the lick.

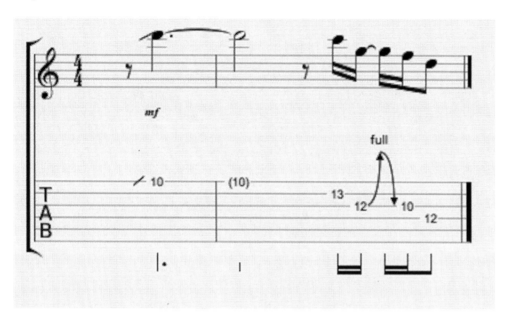

Lick 31: Key of D

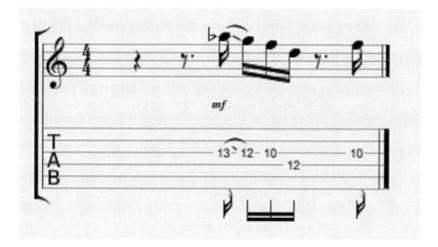

Magic Sam

Lick 32: Key of B

In this lick Magic Sam uses thirds in double stops. Play this this lick in the 9th position and barring with first finger and using middle and ring to play the other thirds.

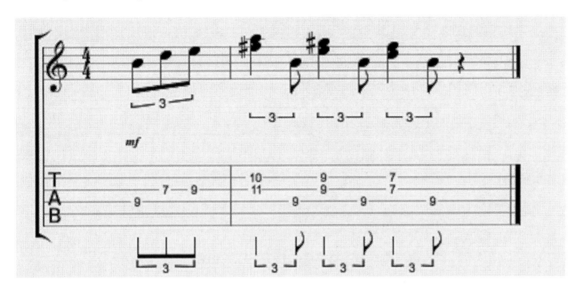

Lick 33: Key of B

This lick features a double bend. Bend the 10th fret up a whole step, and then up a half step. This is a very expressive technique.

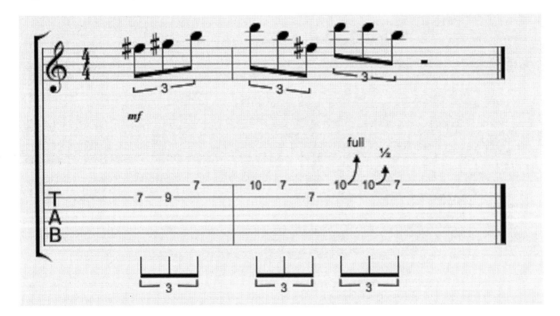

Pat Martino

Lick 34: Key of G

Jazz guitarist, Pat Martino plays a very interesting repeating lick in this example. To play it, use your pinky on the high E string and play the pull offs with either ring or middle and the first finger. This lick also features a polyrhythm by playing a two-note phrase in triplets.

Otis Rush

Lick 35: Key of C

This lick (or variations of it) can be heard in many of the great blues guitarists' solos. The idea is to play the 4th and major 3rd alternating, giving it a sus4 sound.

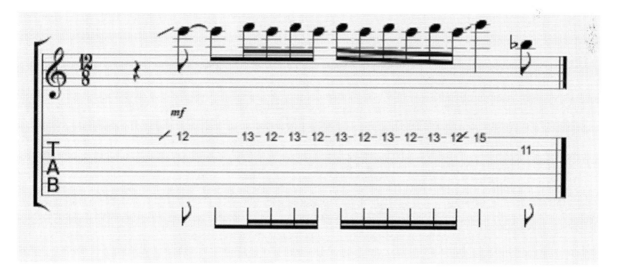

T-Bone Walker

Lick 36: Key of G#

This lick could be considered T-Bone's signature lick. He used it frequently throughout his career. Later, players like Stevie Ray Vaughn used it in his own vocabulary.

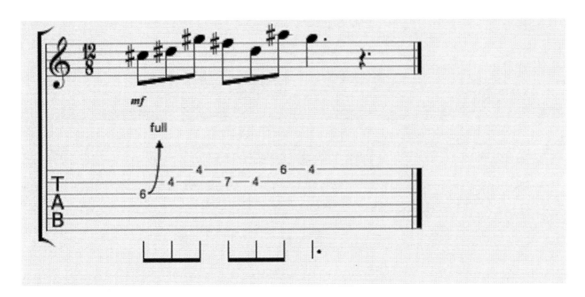

Lick 37: Key of G#

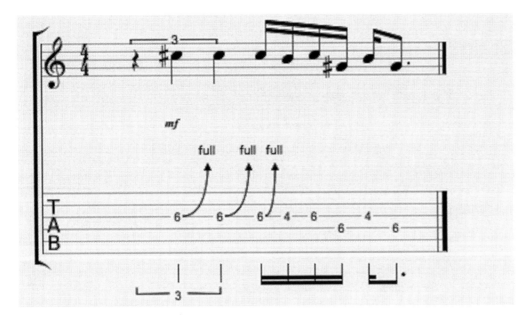

Lick 38: Key of Bb

This repeating lick predates players like Chuck Berry and Jimmy Page by 10 years.

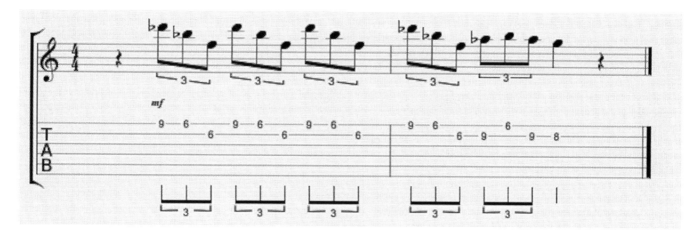

Lick 39: Key of G

This lick comes from one of T-Bone's most famous songs. It is played as an accompanying lick, but would work great in a solo as well.

Muddy Waters

Lick 40: Key of E

Both Lick 40 and 41 feature similar fingerings. These can be traced back to the earlier acoustic blues styles, but work great on the electric guitar as well. Try moving these up the neck into different positions even though they are in the open position.

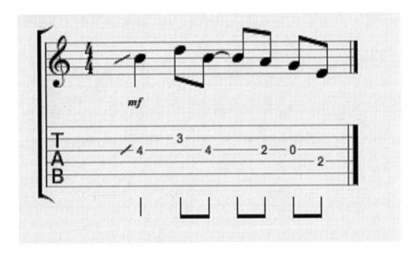

Lick 41: Key of E

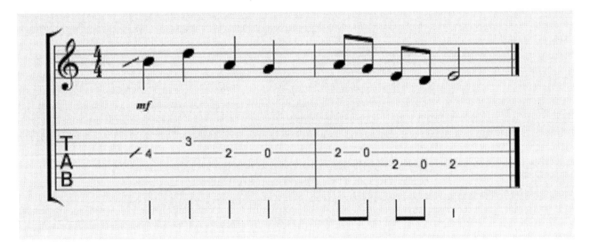

VIII. The IV Chord

The second chord that happens in the blues progression is the IV chord. You will normally find it in bars 5 and 6, but sometimes it will come up in bar 2.

The IV chord is an interesting chord because the key notes of the chord can clash with the key notes of the I chord.

Key of C

I Chord	IV Chord
C	F
E	A
G	C
(Bb)	(Eb)

As you can see in Figure 15 these two chords have 2 notes that differ by a half step.

Another interesting thing about the IV chord is that it contains the 6th note of the scale (for example, A in the key of C), which is not part of the blues or minor pentatonic scales that many players use to solo in a blues setting. Putting that note into your melodies gives you a sound that you are inside the music instead of pasting a scale over top. You will see in many of these examples that they include the 6th degree of the scale.

Duane Allman

Lick 1 : Key of A

This lick uses the 4th and major 3rd and implies the sus4 chord.

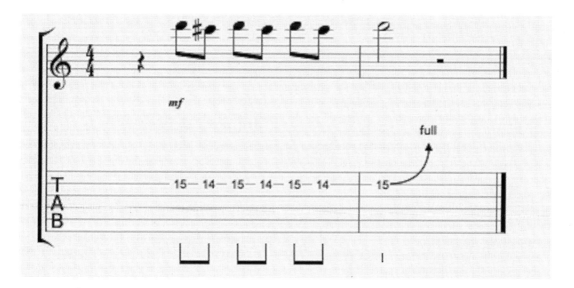

Kenny Burrell

Lick 2: Key of C

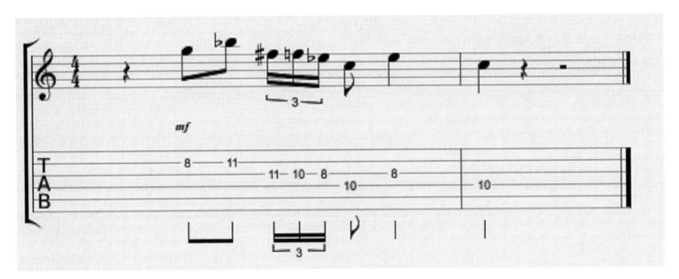

Lick 3: Key of C

This lick is another repeating lick. The great thing about this one is Kenny Burrell's way of getting out of the lick. He slides up to the 4th degree and then follows a minor pentatonic scale down.

Billy Butler

Lick 4: Key of F

In this lick Billy Butler plays a D minor triad, which forms the 3rd, root, and 6th of the I chord. He then lowers the top note to play over the IV chord, giving him the flat 7th, 5th, and 3rd of the Bb7 chord. It's a very interesting lick that can easily be moved around the neck, but is not heard very often.

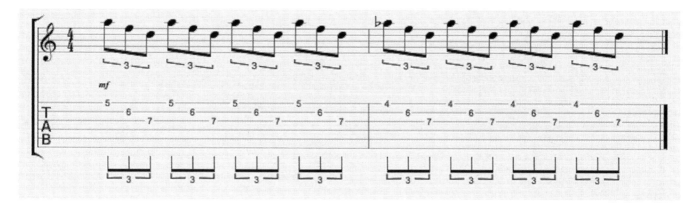

Eric Clapton

Lick 5: Key of C

This lick features a nice sequence in bar 2. The last bar is back in the I chord, which has been left in to show how the lick resolves.

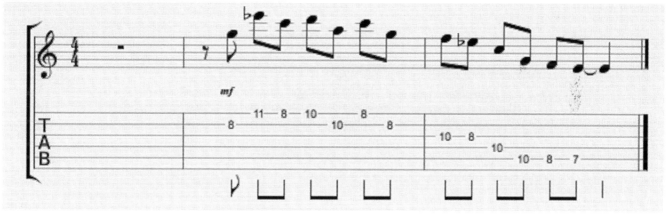

Buddy Guy

Lick 6: Key of F

Buddy Guy uses a type of double bend in this lick where two notes are being bent simultaneously. In this bend the length is not really as important as the effect of the bend itself. Try using ring and pinky to do the bend followed by a small barre on the 13th fret.

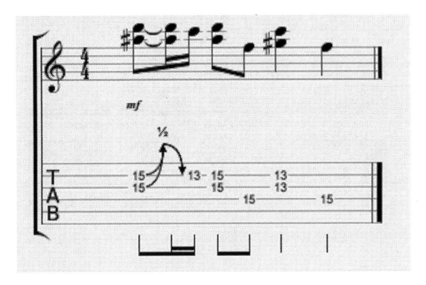

Pat Hare

Lick 7: Key of F

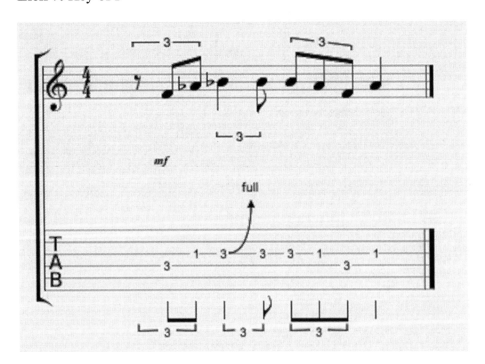

46

Lick 8: Key of F

This lick uses a repeated slide note to start it off. It also uses the 6th of the tonic scale (which is the 3rd of the IV chord – D in this key).

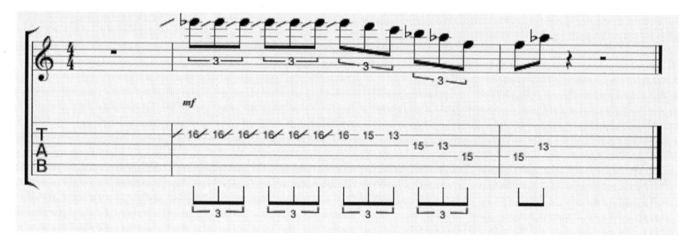

Earl Hooker

Lick 9: Key of D

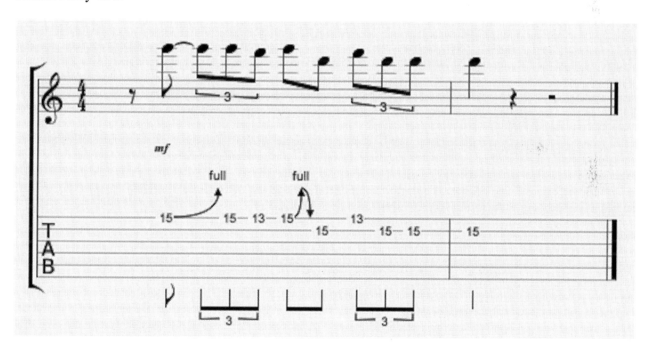

Albert King

Lick 10: Key of Bb

This lick is one of Albert King's classic moves – the major third bend. He typically plays this on the IV chord, bending the flat 7th of that chord up to the 9th. Make sure you use momentum to get this bend to happen instead of trying to muscle it up that far.

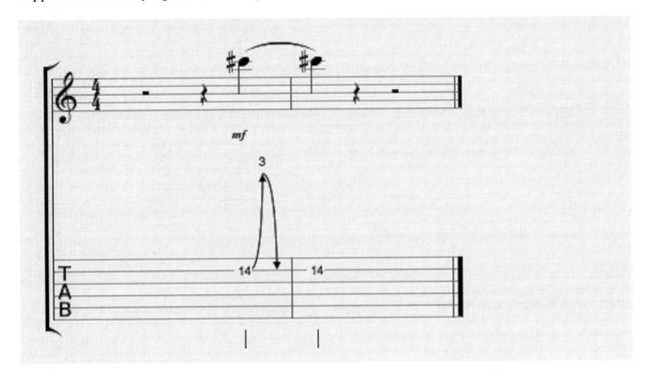

B.B. King

Lick 11: Key of Bb

This lick uses the tritone, which on the IV chord gives you the 3rd and flat 7th. The lick ends on the I chord with major 3rd.

Freddie King

Lick 12: Key of D

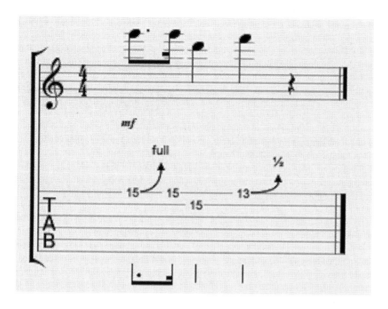

Magic Sam

Lick 13: Key of B

In this lick Magic Sam uses a pretty typical minor pentatonic phrase. The skip at the end of the lick makes it stand out and gives it more of a forward moving feel.

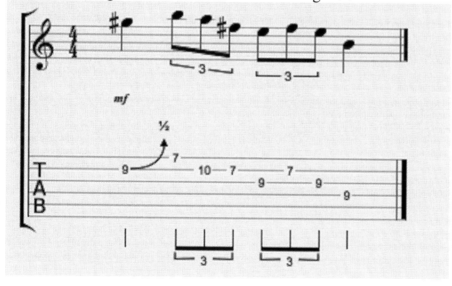

Wes Montgomery

Lick 14: Key of D

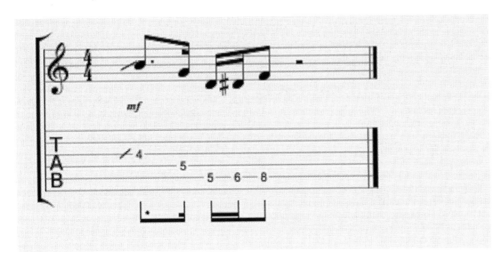

Lick 15: Key of Db

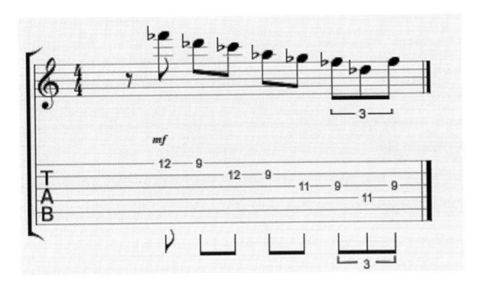

Otis Rush

Lick 16: Key of C

Otis Rush uses a 2 against 3 feel here by playing a two-note phrase using triplets. Notice that he also is using the 6th of the key, or the 3rd of the IV chord (A), which helps to ground the sound to the IV chord here.

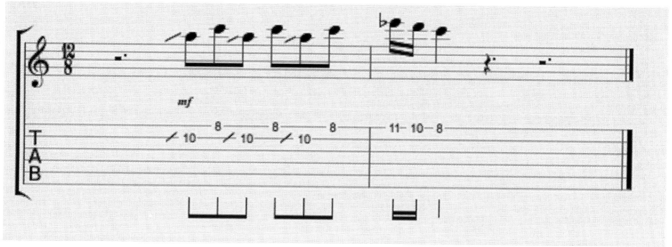

Muddy Waters

Lick 17: Key of E

In this lick, Muddy Waters focuses the line around the root of the IV chord. It is a very simple but effective line, one that can be moved up the neck even with the open strings.

Stevie Ray Vaughn

Lick 18: Key of F#

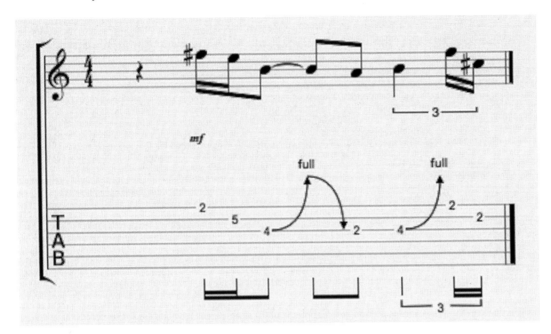

IX. The V Chord

In this study, the V chord section is referring to the 9th and 10th bars of the form. Typically the chord is followed by a IV chord. For that reason the licks here are shown in two bars. Sometimes there will be an entire bar of rest, which means the lick is played over the 10th bar leading back to I.

These licks are all doing one thing, leading back to I. This is where the release happens, and great blues playing is all about the releases.

Duane Allman

Lick 1: Key of D

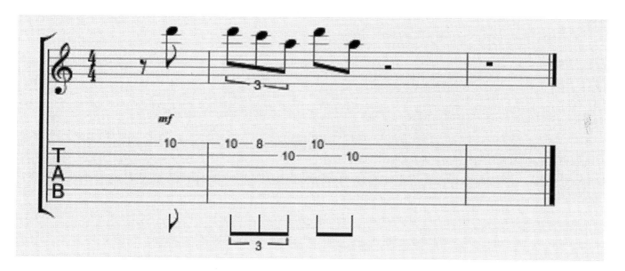

Kenny Burrell

Lick 2: Key of C

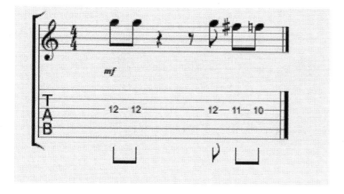

Eric Clapton

Lick 3: Key of C

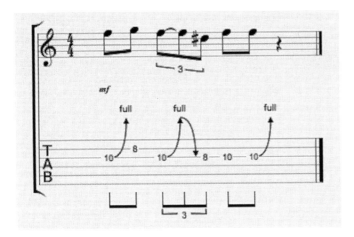

Albert Collins

Lick 4: Key of D

Albert Collins usually used an open minor tuning. The tuning has a big effect on this lick. It's possible to emulate the lick using standard tuning by playing the 6th instead of the flat 7th on the D string. The ending of this lick uses a nice half step bend to imply the major I chord at the end of the lick.

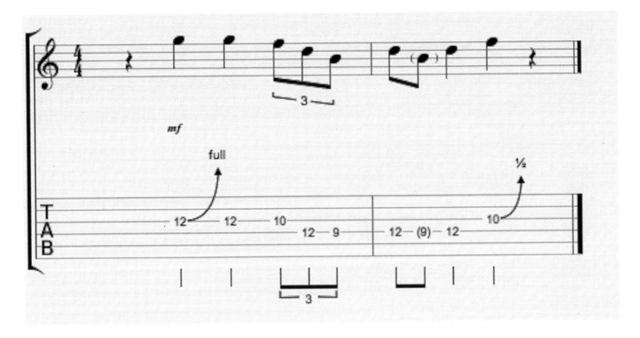

Lick 5: Key of D

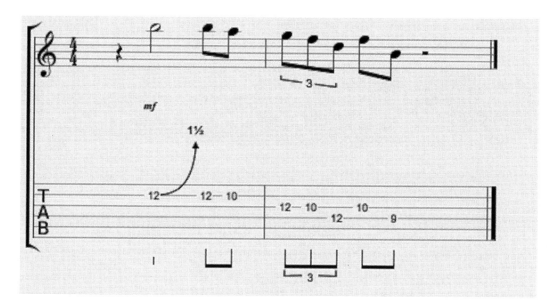

Buddy Guy

Lick 6: Key of A

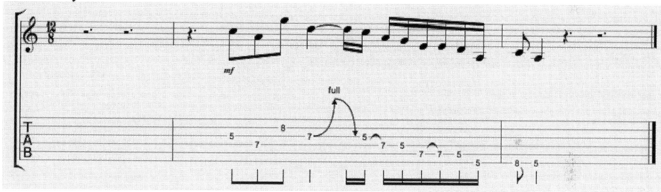

Lick 7: Key of F

This lick is highly chromatic. **Buddy Guy** freely mixes the minor and major 3rds here. The ending wraps things up with the strong minor 3rd note, which gets the ear ready for the IV chord in the next bar.

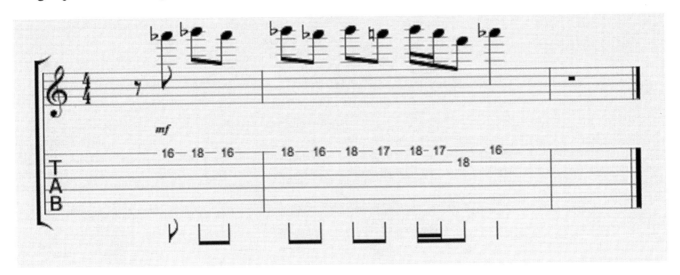

Lick 8: Key of D

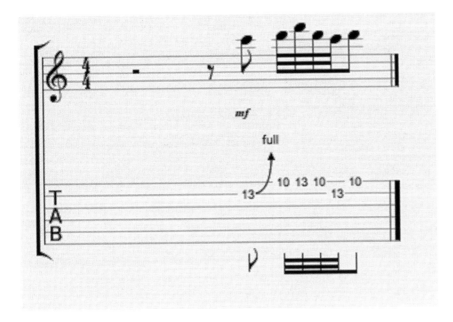

Pat Hare

Lick 9: Key of F

Lick 10: Key of F

This lick uses the 2 against 3 feel that has been featured in the I and IV chord chapters already. The lick is effective because the ending is so strong.

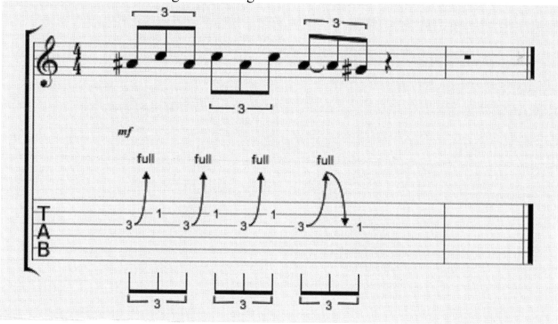

Earl Hooker

Lick 11: Key of D

Here Earl Hooker uses the 6th interval chromatically leading to the 3rd of the key (F#). The lick ends with a nice slide down to the open position. Play the first two doubles stops with middle and ring fingers.

Elmore James

Lick 12: Key of D

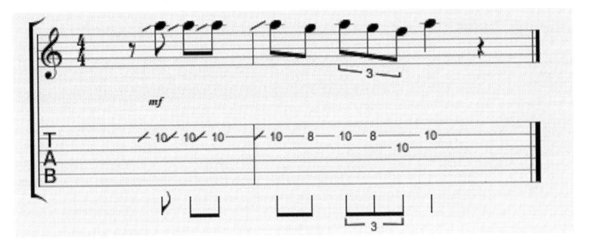

Lick 13: Key of D

In this Elmore James lick you can emulate the slide sound by playing several of the notes like normal, and then sliding back into the same note.

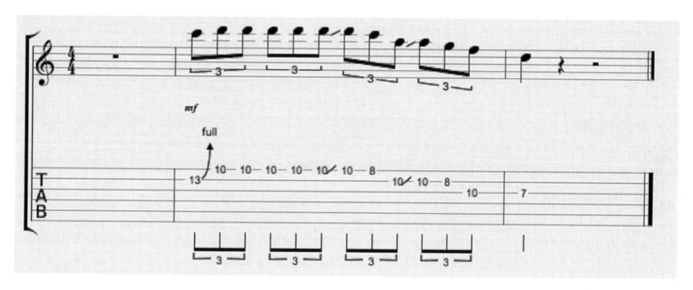

B.B. King

Lick 14: Key of D

This B.B. King lick hints at almost a bebop or jazz line because of its chromaticism. The chromatic notes work well because they outline the chord notes so well. The first full bar has BB moving chromatically down from the 5th to the 3rd of the key, which is then followed by the I triad. The lick ends by chromatically moving to the root of the IV chord.

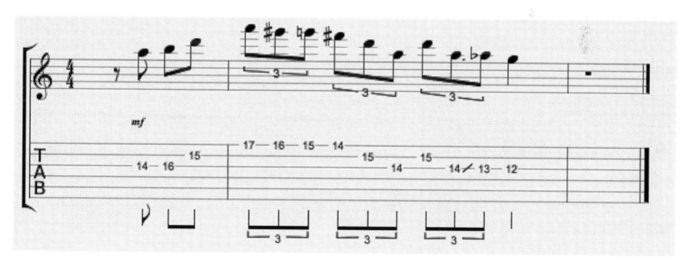

Lick 15: Key of C#

This lick spices up the standard minor pentatonic blues lick by using a hammer on to the major 3rd and later the 9th.

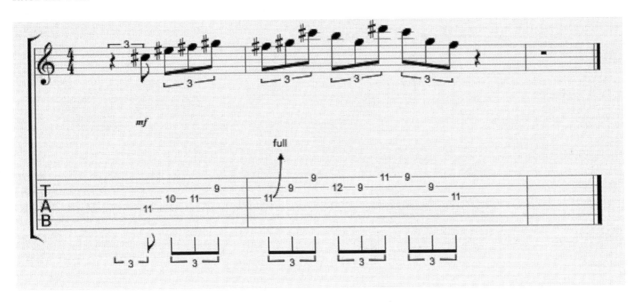

Lick 16: Key of D

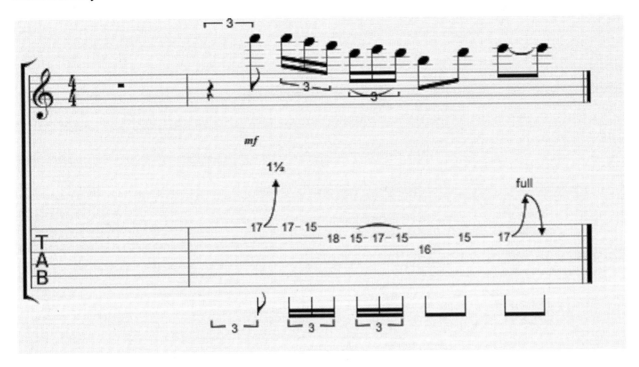

Freddie King

Lick 17: Key of D

This lick features a double bend on the C note – first bent up a minor 3rd then a whole stop. He also plays the note without bending, truly getting the most out of a single note. Make sure to have a good idea of how far to bend up each bend. The first one should sound like a note 3 frets higher (F) while the second should sound 2 frets higher (E).

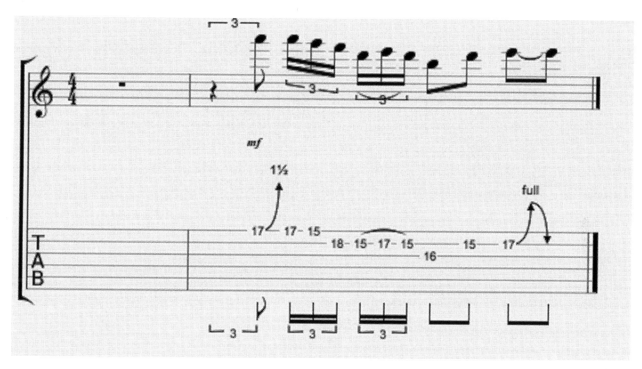

Lick 18: Key of G

Wes Montgomery

T-Bone Walker

Lick 19: Key of G

T-Bone uses a lick similar to the one featured in the I chord. This lick was his bread and butter, some solos using it almost exclusively.

X. Turnaround

The blues form ends with a turnaround. Typically it will be just a I chord followed by a V chord which leads back to the beginning of the form.

The turnaround is one part of the progression that seems to unify many of the soloists. They typically end their lines on the 5th of the key, and that note is usually the bottom note of a triad.

Billy Butler

Lick 1: Key of F

This lick is a rare turnaround lick that ends on the 5th but in the upper register. The beginning of the lick outlines first the F chord, then the Bb7 chord before the half step bend and return to the 5th.

Eric Clapton

Lick 2: Key of C

Clapton plays great turnarounds. Licks 2 and 3 are no exception. They both end with the same phrase. His ability to make simple phrases sound great shows a mastery over the blues language.

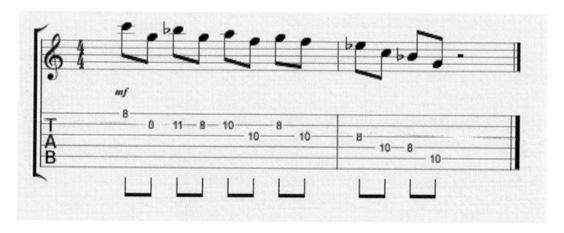

Lick 3: Key of C

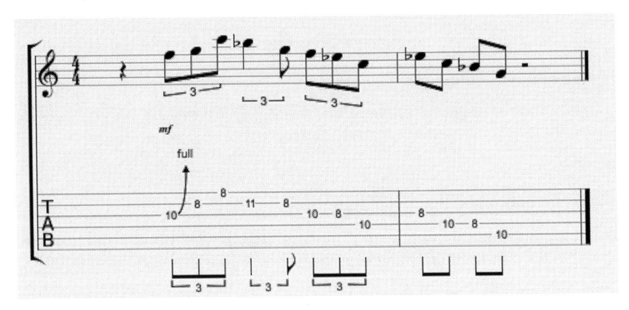

Pat Hare

Lick 4: Key of F

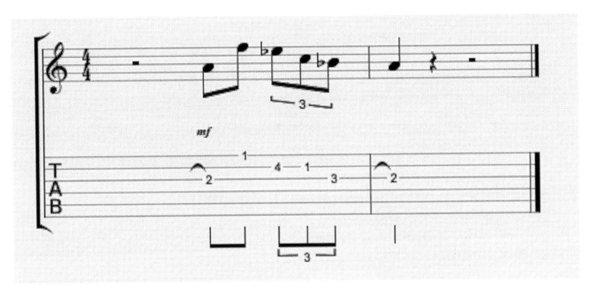

Earl Hooker

Lick 5: Key of D

Earl Hooker uses a technique called sequencing in Lick 5. He is basically taking a short three-note phrase and moving it up a fret at a time before reaching the 5th. He ends the lick with a full triad on the V chord.

B.B. King

Lick 6: Key of D

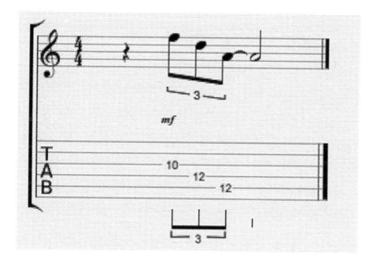

Lick 7: Key of C#

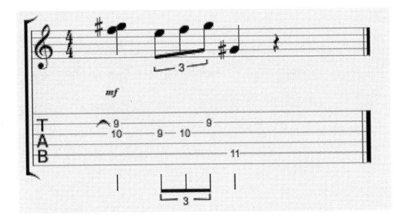

Lick 8: Key of C#

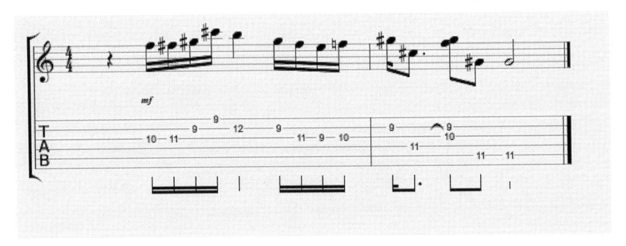

Freddie King

Lick 9: Key of C

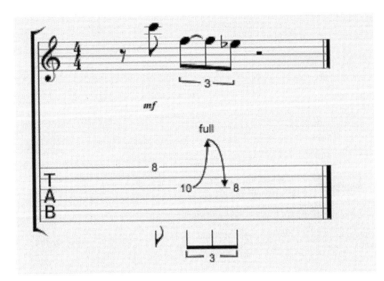

Magic Sam

Lick 10: Key of E

Magic Sam plays a lick here that is more typical in acoustic blues playing. It also works great in the electric style and is an essential one to add to your bag of tricks.

Wes Montgomery

Lick 11: Key of D

Wes plays a very chromatic line here, which is really based on the D major chord (the I chord) until the very end with the 5th of the scale.

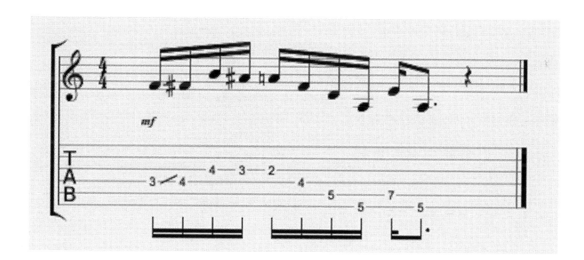

Jimmy Rogers

Lick 12: Key of F

This lick has a great pull from the 2 against 3 feel in the first measure. Rogers ends the lick with a jump from the 3rd down to the 5th of the I chord, which is a very typical move in the turnaround.

Otis Rush

Lick 13: Key of C

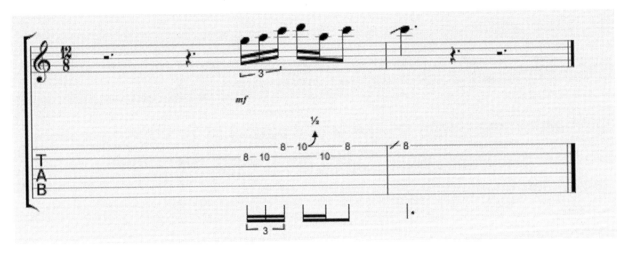

T-Bone Walker

Lick 14: Key of Bb

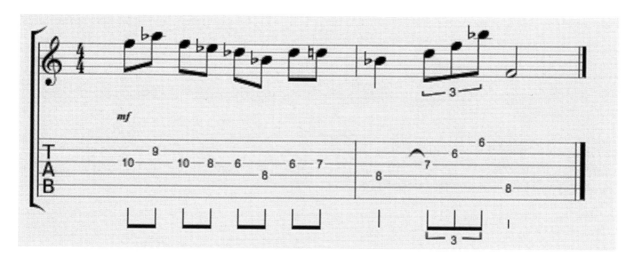

XI. Endings

Every good thing comes to an end, and blues tunes are no different. The ending is one area that sometimes gets overlooked – "We'll worry about it when we get there."

It is important to have a number of endings at your disposal. Many of the masters make it look easy, almost like they're just pulling something out of thin air. That happens because they have taken the time to learn, copy, or come up with a number of different endings.

You will see similarities here. Most of the endings use chromatic motion. The licks will resolve by way of chromatic chords. In these cases the players are using the same chord fingering for both the set up and the resolution. Also, many of them end on the 'and' after beat two.

Eric Clapton

Lick 1 : Key of C

Eric Clapton plays a line that mainly outlines the major pentatonic scale using a bend on the D to hint at the flat 3rd. The lick ends in typical blues fashion (which you will see throughout this chapter) of playing a dominant 9th chord on the flat 2nd moving down to the tonic chord.

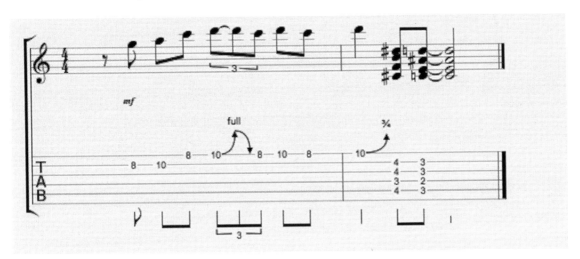

Buddy Guy

Lick 2: Key of A

This lick is an interesting ending to a tune. It is based on a simple chord shape moving chromatically down three times in a row. Hold the last one out to end the tune.

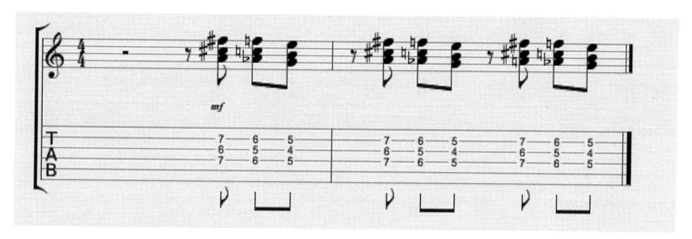

Elmore James

Lick 3: Key of A

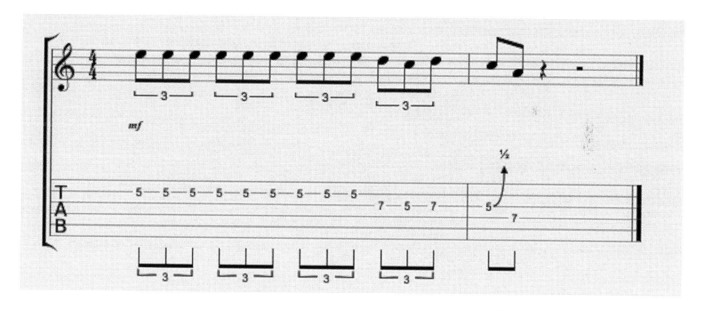

B.B. King

Lick 4: Key of Ab

This lick could also be used in the turnaround section because it ends on the 5th degree of the scale.

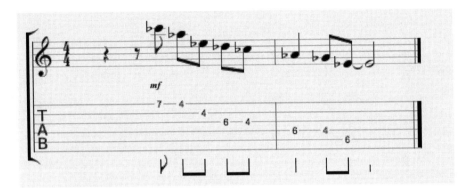

Lick 5: Key of D

B.B. King hints at the b2 to tonic ending with this ending, but does it with single notes rather than whole chords. The rest of the lick comes from the minor pentatonic scale.

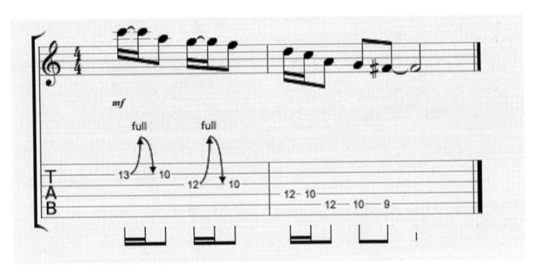

Lick 6: Key of C

Both Lick 6 and 7 end with a similar idea. They are both lines that end with a hammer on into the major 3rd of the key followed by a b2 to tonic chord.

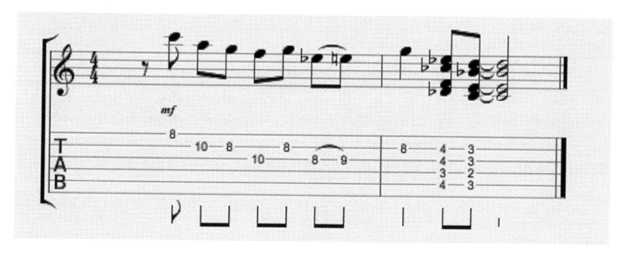

Lick 7: Key of Bb

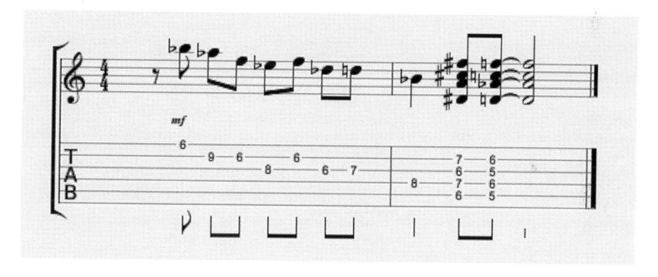

Freddie King

Lick 8: Key of C

This lick has a great bend at the beginning, where Freddie King bends the 2nd up to the 3rd note of the scale. He then bends the flat 3rd up to the 4th.

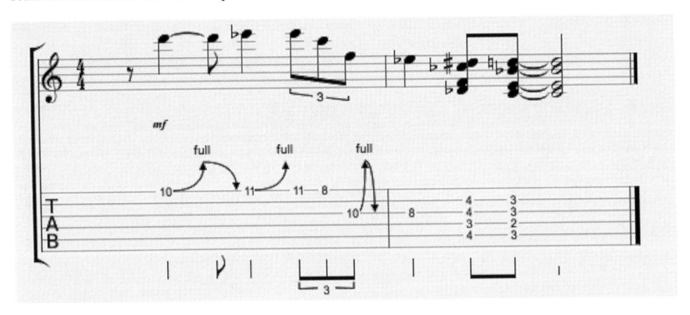

Jimmy Rogers

Lick 9: Key of F

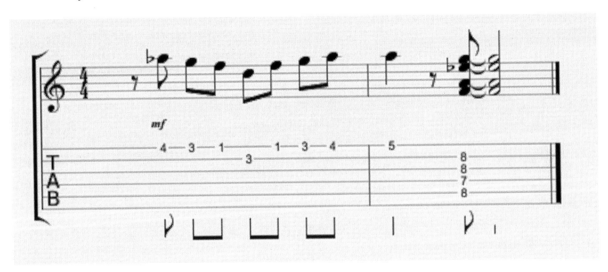

XII. Etude Solos

Applying licks can be a huge obstacle for many musicians trying to learn a new musical language. Books like this one can be inspiring at one level and then leave a lot of room for application.

One of the best ways to apply small musical phrases is to make them into your own etude. This means combining several of them into a solo that you can practice to absorb the licks and phrases.

By writing and learning an etude you begin to make the licks your own. As you play the etude the licks start to work their way into your own playing.

This is a great way to learn the language, but is not the ending point. You wouldn't necessarily want to perform this way – by stringing several licks back to back. But *practicing* this way gives you real – world experience in playing these licks.

Etude #1

The first etude is an example of a 12 bar blues solo in the key of C. The first I chord section uses lick 36 from T-Bone Walker, lick 17 from Pat Hare, and lick 8 from Eric Clapton. Both licks 36 and 17 are re-used in the second I chord section (bars 7 and 8). The IV chord features another Pat Hare lick, this time lick 8 from that section. The V chord has a great lick from Buddy Guy, number 6. Finally the turnaround in the etude comes from lick 4, again by Pat Hare.

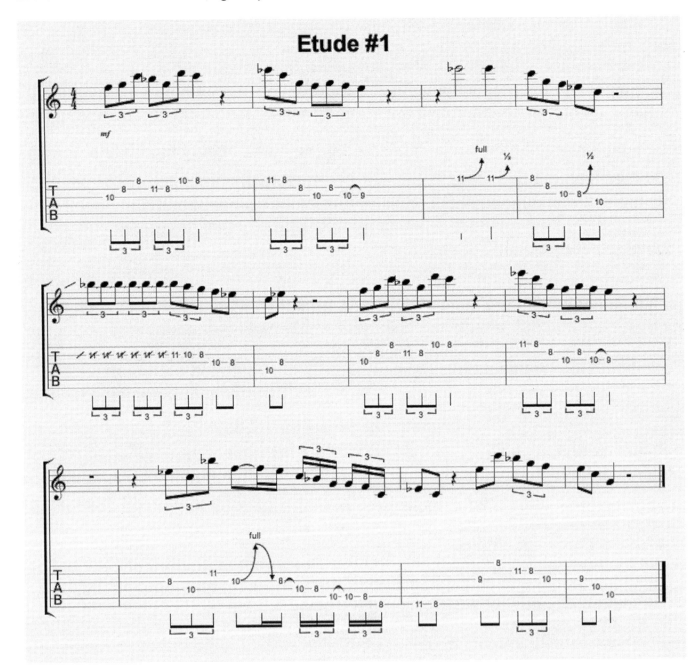

Etude #2

The second etude we will look at is also in the key of C. This time we have an ending instead of a turnaround. It also contains a lick that wasn't covered in the book, just to demonstrate a way to link different licks together if needed. As you learn these (and some readers are probably already well-versed in the blues) you will be able to come up with your own licks that are 'stylistically correct,' or things that sound at home in the blues.

This etude starts with lick 28 from B.B. King, followed by lick 32 by Magic Sam. The IV chord section has another B.B. King lick, this time number 11. This one resolves in bar 7 so we do not need to put a I chord lick there. Lick 7 from the V chord section by Buddy Guy starts out the V chord. Bar 10, which is the second chord in that section is an originally lick. The ending is from lick 5 by B.B. King. Notice that this lick has been adjusted from its original form to help it fit better in context. It has been displaced by two beats. The very end uses a classic bII to I move taken from many of the other ending licks as well as countless tunes.

Variations

In order to create more personalized etudes you can use variations of the licks. Here are a few ideas to help you come up with your variations.

Placement

The premise of this study is to put licks in particular places. You can move them around, though. Try putting the licks in different places in the bar. You can also try putting licks that normally start on the beat off the beat or vice versa. This can create a really interesting rhythmic stretch, which may or may not be what you're going for. The idea though, is to get ideas on creating your own variations.

Rhythmic Variation

Rhythmic variation is simply changing the rhythm. You might lengthen or shorten a series of notes, or just one note. You can also use triplets or eighth notes where they aren't in the original lick.

Editing

Editing phrases and licks is one of the most powerful variation tools. When you edit a lick, you take parts of it out. Sometimes the beginning doesn't fit what you are trying to play. Other times a middle or ending doesn't fit. Maybe just a note or two won't work. Be liberal with editing, it can really change the character of a lick.

Answer

Answering a lick is coming up with a complimentary lick that works with the original. Answering can be very subjective, so be creative when coming up with answers to licks.

Create an Etude

You should work at creating your own etudes, both in blues or any style of music that you're trying to learn. You will absorb the licks by learning and playing your own etude, but the process of creating one teaches you about how to construct a solo. Once you've gone through that process a number of times you begin to do it naturally when playing.

Remember the Music

In the end it's all about the music. No one ultimately cares if you're using lick 18 or 3, listeners just want to hear music. So try not to get weighed down in the minor details presented here. They are only tools to help you improve your playing and understand a different style of guitar playing.

XIII. Discography

The licks in this book are all inspired by the recordings listed here. While this list is a great representation of classic blues recordings, it is not meant to be a complete discography.

Each listing is organized by artist and guitarist, then the album title. Finally, each listing has specific songs that many of the examples are taken from.

Compilations have been used in cases where finding a conventional release is difficult or impossible. Recordings marked with a * are compilations and really, any good compilation of that artist will give a good picture of their guitar playing.

The Allman Brothers (Duane Allman), *Live at the Fillmore*, "Statesboro Blues" "Trouble No More"
Bobby Blue Bland (with **Pat Hare**), *Classic Blues 1952-1962*, "Farther Up The Road" *
Kenny Burrell, *Midnight Blue*, "Chitlins Con Carne"
Billy Butler, *Night Life*, "Honky Tonk"
Eric Clapton, *From the Cradle*, "I'm Tore Down"
Albert Collins, *Truckin'*, "Frosty"
Buddy Guy, *A Man and the Blues*, "Money (That's What I Want)"
Buddy Guy, *The Complete Chess Studios*
Earl Hooker, *Wild Moments – Essential Blues*, "Blues in D Natural" *
Elmore James, *Dust My Broom*, "Dust My Broom" *
Albert King, *King of the Blues Guitar*, "Born Under a Bad Sign"
Albert King, *Live Wire/Blues Power*
B.B. King, *Singing the Blues/The Blues*, "Everyday (I Have the Blues)" "Blind Love"
B.B. King, *Live at Cook County Jail*
B.B. King, *Completely Well*
Freddie King, *The Ultimate Collection*, "Going Down" *
Magic Sam, *West Side Soul*, "All My Loving" "Sweet Home Chicago"
Pat Martino, *El Hombre*, "Blues for Mickey-O"
John Mayall and the Bluesbreakers (Eric Clapton), *Bluesbreakers with Eric Clapton*, "Hideaway"
Wes Montgomery, *The Incredible Jazz Guitar*, "D Natural Blues"
Jimmy Rogers, *Chicago Bound*, "You're the One"
Otis Rush, *Door to Door*, "So Close"
T-Bone Walker, *American Blues Legend*, "Bobby Sox Blues" "They Call it Stormy Monday" *
Muddy Waters, *At Newport 1960*, "Got My Mojo Working"
Muddy Waters, *Folk Singer*
Junior Wells (with Buddy Guy), *Hoodoo Man Blues*, "Hoodoo Man Blues"
Junior Wells (with Elmore James), *Blues Hits Big Town*, "Hoodoo Man Blues"

Conclusion

I hope you have learned a lot about the blues and learning a different musical language. As you can see I feel that it's one of the most important things in learning a musical style.

Make sure to put this material to good use right away. Create etudes and try placing these licks in different situations. You have to use this material for it to make a difference.

I would love to hear about your progress and any questions you may have as you go through the book. Please feel free to send me an email at sam@samsmileymusic.com.

Thank you for purchasing this book, I cannot tell you how much gratitude I have towards everyone who has bought the book.

About Sam Smiley

Sam Smiley is a Midwest-based guitarist who is searching for the meeting place between different American music styles and approaches. He has spent considerable time working with the jazz and country music traditions, finding a meeting place in his recent project, Shikane. He has been described by world class guitarist, Fareed Haque, as a blend of Bill Frisell and Hank Garland.

He also leads the band, Shikane which is scheduled to release their first album "That Would Make Some Sense" in 2014,

As a freelance guitarist, Sam has performed with and recorded with a variety of bands. He has also had the opportunity to travel the US and Europe for performances. He has written articles for Just Jazz Guitar Magazine, Making Music Magazine, and Mel Bay's Sessions. His second eBook, Blues Language is a study of contextually applying phrases from the blues masters. His first eBook, I'll Be All Smiles Tonight, was released in the fall of 2011. It is an exploration of Luther Perkins' guitar style (Johnny Cash's guitarist).

Appendix

These licks were all part of the Facebook campaign leading up to the release of this eBook. There is no commentary here, just the licks and keys presented in each section of the blues form.

The I Chord

Duane Allman

Lick 1: Key of A

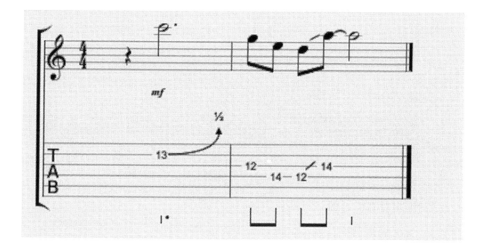

Kenny Burrell

Lick 2: Key of C

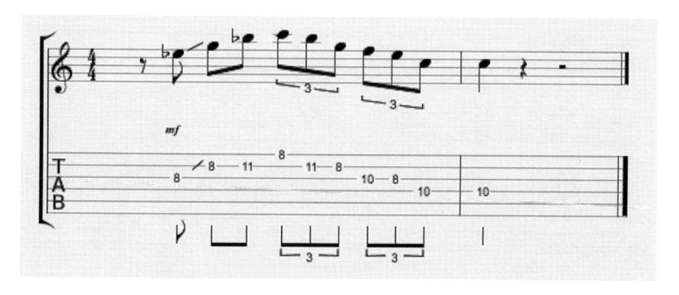

Lick 3: Key of C

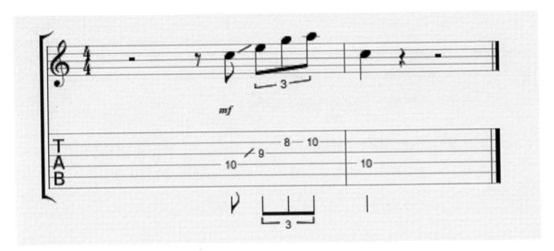

Billy Butler

Lick 4: Key of F

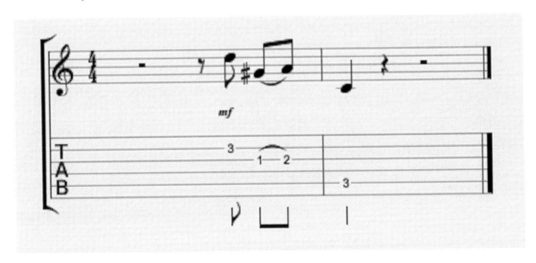

Eric Clapton

Lick 5: Key of C

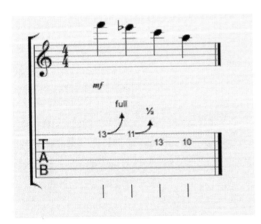

Lick 6: Key of C

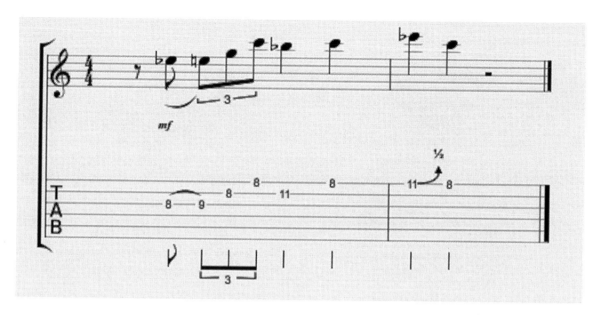

Pat Hare

Lick 7: Key of F

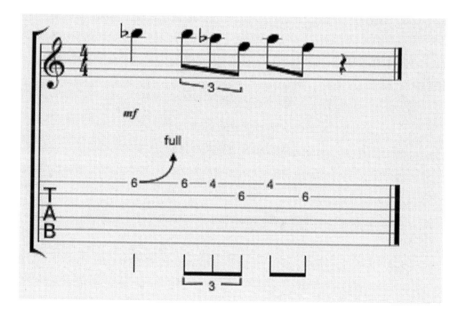

Buddy Guy

Lick 8: Key of F

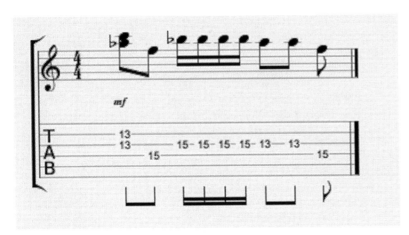

Earl Hooker

Lick 9: Key of D

Albert King

Lick 10: Key of Bb

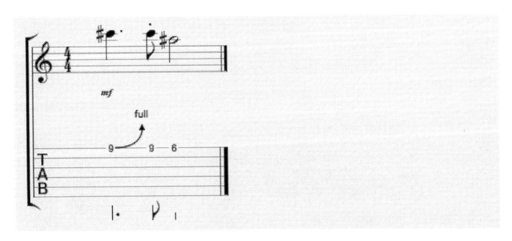

Lick 11: Key of G

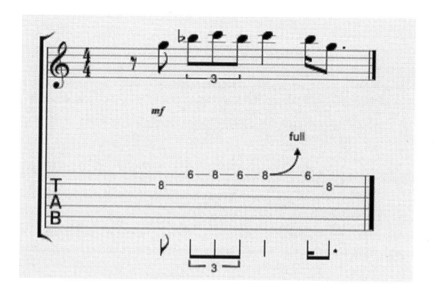

B.B. King

Lick 12: Key of C#

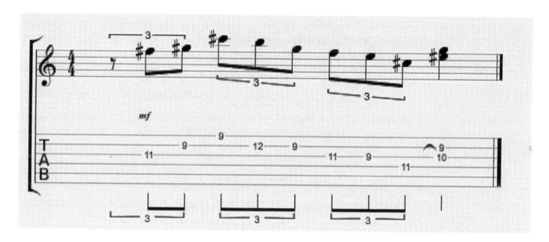

Lick 13: Key of C#

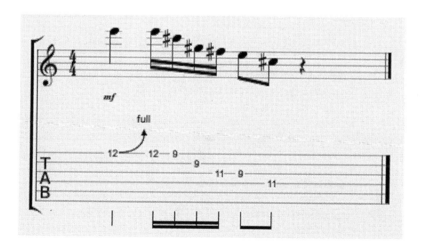

Lick 14: Key of Bb

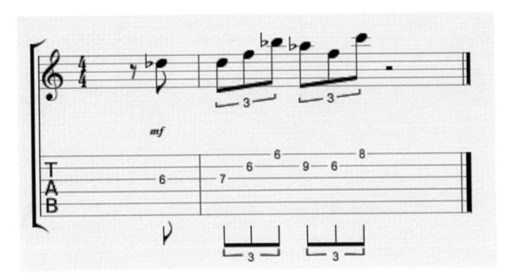

Freddie King

Lick 15: Key of D

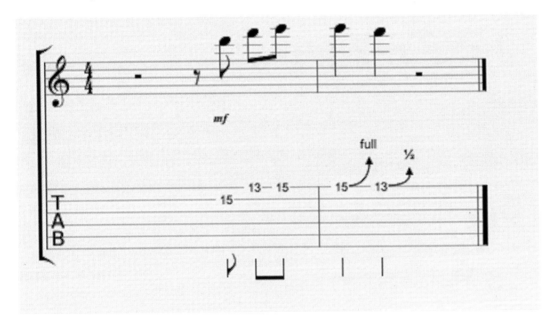

Pat Martino

Lick 16: Key of G

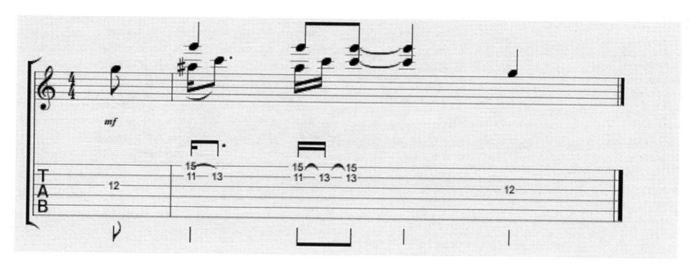

Wes Montgomery

Lick 17: Key of Db

T-Bone Walker

Lick 18: Key of G

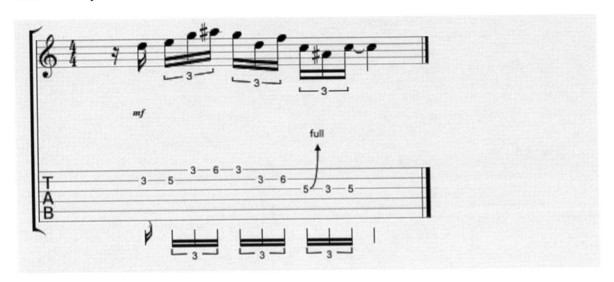

The IV Chord

Buddy Guy

Lick 19: Key of F

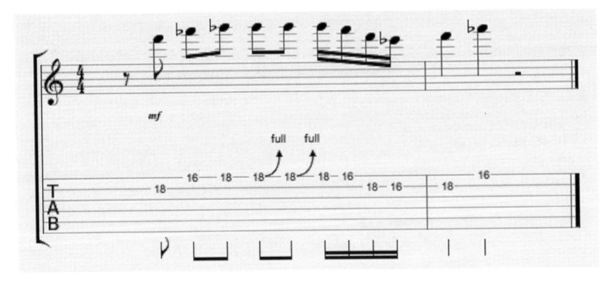

Earl Hooker

Lick 20: Key of D

Magic Sam

Lick 21: Key of D

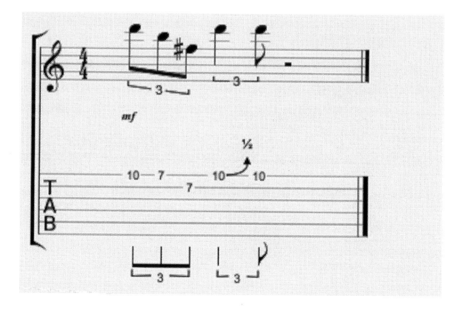

The V Chord

Eric Clapton

Lick 22: Key of C

B.B. King

Lick 23: Key of C#

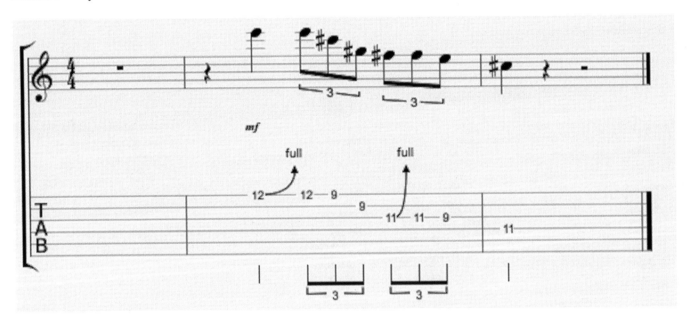

Turnaround

Eric Clapton

Lick 24: Key of C

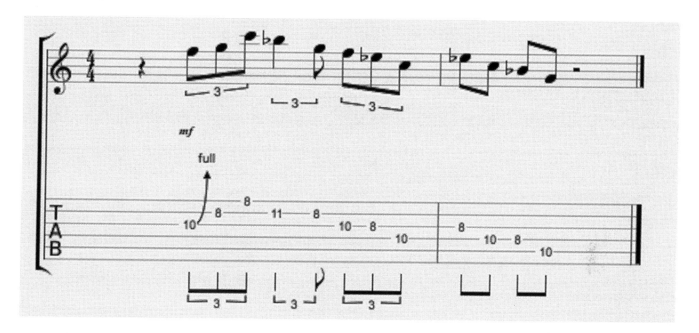

Endings

Pat Hare

Lick 25: Key of F

Contact Details

All the audio examples in this book are available for free download from

http://www.samsmileymusic.com/bluesaudio/

To get in touch with the author please visit www.samsmileymusic.com

Be social; get regular free lessons on facebook: www.facebook.com/samsmileymusic

and keep up to the minute with twitter: twitter.com/samsmileymusic

Made in the USA
San Bernardino, CA
15 August 2018